CRYPTOCURRENCY

CRYPTOCURRENCY

Know How Digital Money Works

Rayoly Services

Raymundo Ramírez

CRYPTOCURRENCY

Copyright 2018 Raymundo Ramírez

All the rights are reserved.

Country of publication: United States of America

TABLE OF CONTENTS

INTRODUCTION

Chapter 1

COINS YOU SHOULD BE AWARE OF---------------------------------11

Chapter 2

THE BASICS OF CRYPTOCURRENCY AND THE WAY IT WORKS--13

Chapter 3

UNDERSTANDING BITCOIN BASICS---------------------------------19

Chapter 4

WHAT IS BLOCKCHAIN AND HOW IT WORKS--------------------39

Chapter 5

HOW TO TRADE CRYPTOCURRENCIES, The Basics of Investing in Digital Currencies---67

Chapter 6

WHAT CRYPTOCURRENCIES ARE GOOD TO INVEST IN-------77

Chapter 7

INCREDIBLE BENEFITS OF THE CRYPTOCURRENCY----------85

Chapter 8

THE FUTURE OF CRIPTOCURRENCY-------------------------------91

CONCLUSION--93

ABOUT THE AUTHOR.

INTRODUCTION

Cryptocurrency is an electronic money created with technology controlling its creation and protecting transactions, while hiding the identities of its users.

Crypto - is short for "cryptography", and cryptography is computer technology used for security, hiding information, identities and more.

Cryptocurrencies are digital cash designed to be quicker, cheaper and more reliable than our regular government issued money. Instead of trusting a government to create your money and banks to store, send and receive it, users transact directly with each other and store their money themselves.

Bitcoin was created as a peer to peer electronic cash system. It is a decentralized network of computers that stores transactions in a ledger, in the form of a blockchain. Bitcoin was created as an open-source project, which means the code was visible from the first day to the whole world to examine, copy, and modify.

Since Bitcoin's inception in January 2009, there have been thousands of other projects that used similar ideas as Bitcoin. These are collectively referred to as "cryptocurrencies". Some of these projects are not necessarily geared towards a currency application, but they are all 'tokens', like Bitcoin. They can be transferred from one user to another, and can usually be traded on an exchange.

Currently there are over 600 cryptocurrencies traded on the markets, tracked by Coinmarketcap. Bitcoin makes up over 80% of the total market today. Cryptocurrencies other than Bitcoin are usually traded against Bitcoin. Some of the larger ones are also traded against government-backed currencies like US Dollar and Chinese Yuan.

Cryptocurrencies, by their nature, are public for anyone to join and participate. They differ significantly in terms of details, such as the consensus protocol used by the network to agree on the list of valid transactions, the way transaction and account information is stored, the specific algorithms used for hashing, the type of public-private key cryptography, the real-world applications and use cases and the type of community.

To prevent fraud and manipulation, every user of a cryptocurrency can simultaneously record and verify their own transactions and the transactions of everyone else. The digital transaction recordings are known as a "ledger" and this ledger is publicly available to anyone.

Each transaction is recorded on a digital record kept by many people across the world known as the "blockchain". The data on the blockchain is publicly available and stored on many computers. There are so many copies being simultaneously maintained, the transaction and banking data is very safe and virtually impossible to manipulate.

Blockchain - Blockchain is technology for creating permanent, secure digital recordings that don't rely on any single person or group. Blockchains can record any information. It is a block, and can record anything. Blocks are created one after the other, chained to each other creating what we know as the blockchain.

Mining - Mining is the computer process of recording and verifying information on the digital record known as the blockchain. Because mining requires computer power, people do this work in return for money. Each computer that fulfills this process can earn a reward in digital money.

Chapter 1

COINS YOU SHOULD BE AWARE OF

1. **Bitcoin** - The first and most popular traded cryptocurrency. Because of its popularity, it has become an anchor in the cryptocurrency market. That means, as the price of bitcoin goes up and down, the prices of other cryptocurrencies move around too.

2. **Ethereum** - The second largest cryptocurrency. Ethereum is built with publicly available software that developers can use to build their own cryptocurrency and software. Some cryptocurrencies built with it include: OMG, QTUM, EOS, and BAT. Some of the apps built from it include games, social networks, and marketplaces.

3. **Ripple** - A cryptocurrency with technology that allows organizations such as banks and companies to securely and instantly send money at almost no cost.

4. **Litecoin** - Litecoin is the silver to bitcoin's gold, meaning it's way less expensive. Litecoin is a cryptocurrency based on bitcoin's technology with improvements to transaction speed, and a reduction of transaction cost. Unlike bitcoin, litecoin focuses on using the latest in technology to improve performance and user experience.

5. **Neo** - Neo is a Chinese cryptocurrency that has similar technology to Ethereum allowing developers to build their own cryptocurrency. Because ethereum is #2 in the crypto universe, comparing neo to it has boosted neo's value. The first coin being developed with NEO is Redpulse.

Chapter 2

THE BASICS OF CRYPTOCURRENCY AND THE WAY IT WORKS

Cryptocurrency is nothing but digital currency, which has been designed to impose security and anonymity in online monetary transactions. It uses cryptographic encryption to both generate currency and verify transactions. The new coins are created by a process called mining, whereas the transactions are recorded in a public ledger, which is called the Transaction Block Chain.

Little Backtrack

Evolution of cryptocurrency is mainly attributed to the virtual world of the web and involves the procedure of transforming legible information into a code, which is almost uncrackable. Thus, it becomes easier to track purchases and transfers involving the currency. Cryptography, since its introduction in the WWII to secure communication, has evolved in this digital age, blending with mathematical theories and computer science. Thus, it is now used to secure not only communication and information but also money transfers across the virtual web.

How To Use Cryptocurrency

It is very easy for the ordinary people to make use of this digital currency. Just follow the steps given below:

You need a digital wallet (obviously, to store the currency) Make use of the wallet to create unique public addresses (this enables you to receive the currency)

Use the public addresses to transfer funds in or out of the wallet Cryptocurrency Wallets

A cryptocurrency wallet is nothing else than a software program, which is capable to store both private and public keys. In addition to that, it can also interact with different blockchains, so that the users can send and receive digital currency and also keep a track on their balance.

The Way The Digital Wallets Work

In contrast to the conventional wallets that we carry in our pockets, digital wallets do not store currency. In fact, the concept of blockchain has been so smartly blended with cryptocurrency that the currencies never get stored at a particular location. Nor do they exist anywhere in hard cash or physical form. Only the records of your transactions are stored in the blockchain and nothing else.

A Real-Life Example

Suppose, a friend sends you some digital currency, say in form of bitcoin. What this friend does is he transfers the ownership of the coins to the address of your wallet. Now, when you want to use that money, you've unlock the fund.

In order to unlock the fund, you need to match the private key in your wallet with the public address that the coins are assigned to. Only when both these private and public addresses match, your account will be credited and the balance in your wallet will swell. Simultaneously, the balance of the sender of the digital currency will decrease. In transactions related to digital currency, the actual exchange of physical coins never take place at any instance.

Understanding The Cryptocurrency Address

By nature, it is a public address with a unique string of characters. This enables a user or owner of a digital wallet to receive cryptocurrency from others. Each public address, that is generated, has a matching private address. This automatic match proves or establishes the ownership of a public address. As a more practical analogy, you may consider a public cryptocurrency address as your eMail address to which others can send emails. The emails are the currency that people send you.

Understanding the latest version of technology, in form of cryptocurrency is not tough. One needs a little interest and spend time on the net to get the basics clear.

Capitulo 3

UNDERSTANDING BITCOIN BASICS

For someone not familiar with Bitcoin, the first question that comes to mind is, "What is Bitcoin?" And another common question that is often asked relates to the Bitcoin price. It started out a under 10 cents per Bitcoin upon its introduction in early 2009. It has risen steadily since and has hovered around $4000 per Bitcoin recently. So regarding Bitcoin value or the Bitcoin rate this is a most remarkable appreciation of value and has created many, many millionaires over the last eight years.

Bitcoin is a form of currency existing only in the digital world. The technology was created by an individual hiding under an identity named Satoshi Nakamoto. To this day, the creator/creators of the system never materialized, maintaining an anonymous status.

Bitcoins are not printed like traditional currencies as there are no physical representations for the cryptocurrency; it is produced by users and numerous businesses through a process called mining. This is where dedicated software solves mathematical problems in exchange for the virtual currency.

A user takes control of it using electronic devices, which also serves as medium to complete transactions with the help of numerous platforms. It is also kept and secured with the employment of virtual wallets.

The Bitcoin market is worldwide and the citizens of China and Japan have been particularly active in its purchase along with other Asian countries. However, recently in Bitcoin news the Chinese government has tried to suppress its activity in that country. That action drove the value of Bitcoin down for a short time but it soon surged back and is now close to its previous value.

The Bitcoin history chart is very interesting. Its creator was an anonymous group of brilliant mathematicians (using the pseudonym Satoski Nakamoto) who designed it in 2008 to be "virtual gold" and released the first Bitcoin software in early 2009 during the height of the USA economic crisis. They knew that to have lasting value, it like gold had to have a finite supply. So in creating it they capped the supply at 21 million Bitcoin.

Bitcoin mining refers to the process by which new Bitcoin is created. With conventional currency, government decides when and where to print and distribute it. With Bitcoin, "miners" use special software to solve complex mathematical problems and are issued a certain number of Bitcoin in return.

A question that then arises is, is Bitcoin mining worth it. The answer is no for the average person. It takes very sophisticated knowledge and a powerful computer system and this combination of factors makes it unattainable for the masses. This applies even more to bitcoin mining 2017 than in past years.

Many wonder, who accepts Bitcoin? This question gets asked in various ways, what are stores that accept bitcoin, what are websites that accept bitcoins, what are some retailers that accept bitcoin, what are some places that accept bitcoin and where can I spend bitcoin.

More and more companies are beginning to see the value of accepting cryptocurrencies as a valid payment option. Some major companies that do are DISH network, Microsoft, Expedia, Shopify stores, Newegg, Payza, 2Pay4You, and others. Two major holdouts at this time are Walmart and Amazon.

Ethereum is the strongest rival to Bitcoin in the cryptocurrency market and many wonder at the question of Bitcoin vs Ethereum. Ethereum was created in mid-2015 and has gained some popularity but still ranks far behind Bitcoin in usage, acceptance and value.

A question that often comes up often relates to Bitcoin scam. This author has a friend who made a purchase from a company that promised 1-2% growth per day. The company website listed no contact information and after a couple months the website simply vanished one day and my friend lost all the money he had invested which was several thousand dollars.

One has to know how to buy Bitcoins, how to purchase Bitcoin or how to buy Bitcoin with credit card in order to get started. Coinbase is a very popular site to do this. Their fee is 3.75% and the buying limit is $10,000 per day. This would probably be the easiest way to buy bitcoins.

Others would like to buy Bitcoin with debit card. Coinbase also provides this service and has clear step by step instructions on how to proceed with either your debit or credit card. There are those who would like to buy Bitcoin instantly. This can be done at Paxful, Inc. and can be done through W. Union or any credit/debit card.

Other common questions that come up are what is the best way to buy Bitcoins, the best way to get bitcoins or where to buy bitcoins online. The easiest way is probably to purchase it through a digital asset exchange like the previously mentioned Coinbase. Opening an account with them is painless and once you link your bank account with them you can buy and sell Bitcoin quite easily. This is quite likely also the best place to buy Bitcoins.

One must know what a Bitcoin wallet is and how to use it. It is simply the Bitcoin equivalent of a bank account. It allows you to receive Bitcoins, store them and send them to others. What it does is store a collection of Bitcoin privacy keys. Typically it is encrypted with a password or otherwise protected from unauthorized access.

There are several types of digital wallets to choose from. A web wallet allows you to send, receive and store Bitcoin though your web browser. Another type is a desktop wallet and here the wallet software is stored directly on your computer. There are also mobile wallets which are designed for use by a mobile device.

A question that occasionally comes up is that of Bitcoin stock or how to buy Bitcoin stock. By far the most common way to proceed in this area is to buy Bitcoin directly and not its stock.

There is one entity called Bitcoin Investment trust which is an investment fund that is designed to track the market flow of Bitcoin. Some analysts however are calling this a risky way to become involved in this marketplace.

The Bitcoin exchange rate USD is a closely watched benchmark both on a daily basis and long term over the last 8 years since its introduction to the world's financial marketplace. A popular company to receive the most current rate in Bitcoin valuation is XE. They show Bitcoin to USD valuation and also the complete Bitcoin price chart, the Bitcoin value chart and the Bitcoin to USD chart. If you ask, "How much is one Bitcoin?" you will always know from their continuously updated charts.

Similar questions that come up in this area relate to the bitcoin rate history, the bitcoin price chart live, the bitcoin to dollar exchange rate, the bitcoin dollar chart and the bitcoin 5 year chart. The previously mentioned website, xe, is also a good source for answers to these questions.

Regarding Bitcoin cash, ie. to get USD from selling Bitcoin, Bitwol is one company that enables you to do this. WikiHow is another company that will take you through this process.

Bitcoin projected value is a subject often discussed. In January of 2015 the price of one bitcoin was $215. Currently it is around $5000. This is a phenomenal increase and one far beyond what most experts would have projected at that time. Currently in reviewing forecasts from experts around the world a common answer seems to be that the top value will settle in at around $10,000 and one expert even projected a value reaching $100,000.

How Does Bitcoin Work?

Bitcoin is a type of electronic currency (CryptoCurrency) that is autonomous from traditional banking and came into circulation in 2009. According to some of the top online traders, Bitcoin is considered as the best known digital currency that relies on computer networks to solve complex mathematical problems, in order to verify and record the details of each transaction made.

The Bitcoin exchange rate does not depend on the central bank and there is no single authority that governs the supply of CryptoCurrency. However, the Bitcoin price depends on the level of confidence its users have, as the more major companies accept

Bitcoin as a method of payment, the more successful Bitcoin will become.

Benefits And Risks Of Bitcoin

One of the benefits of Bitcoin is its low inflation risk. Traditional currencies suffer from inflation and they tend to lose their purchasing power each year, as governments continue to use quantative easing to stimulate the economy.

Bitcoin doesn't suffer from low inflation, because Bitcoin mining is limited to just 21 million units. That means the release of new Bitcoins is slowing down and the full amount will be mined out within the next couple of decades. Experts have predicted that the last Bitcoin will be mined by 2050.

Bitcoin has a low risk of collapse unlike traditional currencies that rely on governments. When currencies collapse, it leads to hyperinflation or the wipeout of one's savings in an instant.

Bitcoin exchange rate is not regulated by any government and is a digital currency available worldwide.

Bitcoin is easy to carry. A billion dollars in the Bitcoin can be stored on a memory stick and placed in one's pocket. It is that easy to transport Bitcoins compared to paper money. One disadvantage of Bitcoin is its untraceable nature, as Governments and other organisations cannot trace the source of your funds and as such can attract some unscrupulous individuals.

How To Make Money With Bitcoin

Unlike other currencies, there are three ways to make money with Bitcoin, saving, trading and mining. Bitcoin can be traded on open markets, which means you can buy Bitcoin low and sell them high.

Volatility Of Bitcoin

The value of Bitcoin dropped in recent weeks because of the abrupt stoppage of trading in Mt. Gox, which is the largest Bitcoin exchange in the world. According to unverified sources, trading was stopped due to malleability-related theft that was said to be worth more than 744,000. The incident has affected the confidence of the investors to the virtual currency.

According to Bitcoin chart, the Bitcoin exchange rate went up to more than $1,100 last December. That was when more people became aware about the digital currency, then the incident with Mt. Gox happened and it dropped to around $530.

In 2014, We expect exponential growth in the popularity of bitcoin around the world with both merchants and consumers, Stephen Pair, BitPay's co-founder and CTO, anticipate seeing the biggest growth in China, India, Russia and South America.

India has already been cited as the next likely popular market that Bitcoin could move into. Africa could also benefit hugely from using BTC as a currency-of-exchange to get around not having a functioning central bank system or any other country that relies heavily on mobile payments. Bitcoin's expansion in 2014 will be led by Bitcoin ATMs, mobile apps and tools.

World Experiences Bitcoin

More people have accepted the use of Bitcoin and supporters hope that one day, the digital currency will be used by consumers for their online shopping and other electronic deals. Major companies have already accepted payments using the virtual currency. Some of the large firms include Fiverr, TigerDirect and Zynga, among others.

The Future Of Bitcoin

Bitcoin works, but critics have said that the digital currency is not ready to be used by the mainstream because of its volatility. They also point to the hacking of the Bitcoin exchange in the past that has resulted in the loss of several millions of dollars.

Supporters of digital currencies have said that there are newer exchanges that are supervised by financial experts and venture capitalists. Experts added that there is still hope for the virtual currency system and the predicted growth is huge.

Characteristics Of Bitcoin

Bitcoin has the characteristics of traditional currencies such as purchasing power, and investment applications using online trading instruments. It works just like conventional money, only in the sense that it can only exist in the digital world.

One of its unique attributes that cannot be matched by fiat currency is that it is decentralized. The currency does not run under a governing body or an institution, which means it cannot be controlled by these entities, giving users full ownership of their bitcoins.

Moreover, transactions occur with the use of Bitcoin addresses, which are not linked to any names, addresses, or any personal information asked for by traditional payment systems.

Every single Bitcoin transaction is stored in a ledger anyone can access, this is called the blockchain. If a user has a publicly used address, its information is shared for everyone to see, without its user's information of course.

Accounts are easy to create, unlike conventional banks that requests for countless information, which may put its users in jeopardy due to the frauds and schemes surrounding the system.

Furthermore, Bitcoin transactions fees will always be small in number. Apart from near-instant completion of processing, no fees are known to be significant enough to put a dent on one's account.

Uses Of Bitcoin

Apart from its abilities to purchase goods and services, one of its known applications features its use for a number of investment vehicles. This includes Forex, trading Bitcoins, and binary options platforms. Furthermore, brands offer services that revolve around Bitcoin as currency.

Clearly, Bitcoin is as flexible as traditional legal tenders. Its introduction provides every individual with new beneficial opportunities with its ease of use and profit making capabilities.

Understanding Why Bitcoin Is Gaining Popularity In The Binary Options Trading

Now binary options trading brokers also allow you to fund your accounts by using Bitcoins. Bitcoin is a form of digital money, which defers quite remarkably from the other conventional currencies like the dollar and the pound.

Some of the main highlights of Bitcoins are:

It uses peer-to-peer technology, and is not controlled by any central authorities. The transactions are carried out collectively among the involved parties and the network, without any intervention from the central banks. It is free from any kind of interferences or manipulations by the governments, since it is totally decentralized.

It is solely a digital form of currency, and you cannot replace them with their physical form. However, you can quickly exchange them for dollars anytime you like.

The top cap of issuing Bitcoins is limited to 21 millions, which is an average of just 25 coins being mined for every 10 minutes. The pace of mining has slowed down even more in the last 2 years.

Bitcoins has limitations in acceptance, because they are not universally accepted at all stores. However, the prospect of acceptance does look better with its growing popularity. This cryptocurrency has come a long way since its introduction in 2009.

Bitcoins are a bit more complex to understand when compared to the conventional currencies like dollars. Therefore, you will need to gain some technical knowledge about them, especially before using them for online trading

One of the drawbacks of Bitcoins is that the transactions will generally take around 10 minutes to complete, which is unlike the regular currencies where the transactions can be completed immediately. Also, the transactions are irreversible, and the refunding can be done only if the recipient agrees to do so.

Bitcoin allows you to make transactions in an anonymous manner, because you will not have to give your name or address. Like mentioned above, it works with the peer-to-peer system.

Before buying Bitcoins, you will need to install the Bitcoin wallet, on your smartphone or computer. In addition to computer and mobile wallets, you can go for the online wallet too. Each wallet will have a specific address code. For each transaction, 2 pair of keys (public and private) will be generated. This encryption system is very secure.

The Bitcoin balance of each account is public, which means anyone can know about the balance of a particular wallet. However, you will still stay anonymous, because you don't have to give your name or private information for doing transactions.

These days many of the Forex and binary options trading brokers has started accepting Bitcoin as one of the currencies. You can buy and sell it against regular currencies like dollars and pounds.

Bitcoins for binary options trading:

The prices on the Bitcoin chart keep changing according to the supply and demand ratio. In addition to trading on the price fluctuations of this cryptocurrency, you can also use it as a mode of payment for purchasing other currencies too.

However, it is very important for you to choose a reliable binary options broker who allows you to use Bitcoins as one of their accepted currencies. You can check out the broker reviews on the rating sites, before choosing the right platforms for binary options trading.

Chapter 4

WHAT IS BLOCKCHAIN AND HOW IT WORKS

Crypto - what? If you've attempted to dive into this mysterious thing called blockchain, you'd be forgiven for recoiling in horror at the sheer opaqueness of the technical jargon that is often used to frame it. So before we get into what a crytpocurrency is and how blockchain technology might change .

In the simplest terms, a blockchain is a digital ledger of transactions, not unlike the ledgers we have been using for hundreds of years to record sales and purchases. The function of this digital ledger is, in fact, pretty much identical to a traditional ledger in that it records debits and credits between people. That is the core concept behind blockchain; the difference is who holds the ledger and who verifies the transactions.

A distributed database

Imagine an electronic spreadsheet, which is copied umpteen number of times across a computer network. Now, imagine the computer network is designed so smartly that it regularly updates the spreadsheet on its own. This is a broad overview of the Blockchain. Blockchain holds information as a shared database. Moreover, this database gets reconciled continuously.

This approach has its own benefits. It does not allow the database to be stored at any single location. The records in it possess genuine public attribute and can be verified very easily. As there's no centralised version of the records, unauthorised users have no means to manipulate with and corrupt the data. The Blockchain distributed database is simultaneously hosted by millions of computers, making the data easily accessible to almost anyone across the virtual web.

To make the concept or the technology clearer, it is a good idea to discuss the Google Docs analogy.

Google Docs Analogy For Blockchain

After the advent of the eMail, the conventional way of sharing documents is to send a Microsoft Word doc as attachment to a recipient or recipients. The recipients will take their sweet time to go through it, before they send back the revised copy. In this approach, one needs to wait till receiving the return copy to see the changes made to the document. This happens because the sender is locked out from making corrections till the recipient is done with the editing and sends the document back. Contemporary databases do not allow two owners access the same record at the same time. This is how banks maintain balances of their clients or account-holders.

In contrast to the set practice, Google docs allow both the parties to access the same document at the same time. Moreover, it also allows to view a single version of the document to both of them simultaneously. Just like a shared ledger, the Google Docs also acts as a shared document. The distributed part only becomes relevant when the sharing involves multiple users. The Blockchain technology is, in a way, an extension of this concept. However, it is important to point out here that the Blockchain is not meant to share documents. Rather, it is just an analogy, which will help to have clear-cut idea about this cutting-edge technology.

Salient Blockchain Features

Blockchain stores blocks of information across the network, that are identical. By virtue of this feature:

The data or information cannot be controlled by any single, particular entity.

- There can't be no single failure point either.

- The data is hold in a public network, which ensures absolute transparency in the overall procedure.

- The data stored in it cannot be corrupted.

- Demand For Blockchain Developers

As stated earlier, Blockchain technology has a very high application in the world of finance and banking. According to the World Bank, more than US$ 430 billion money transfers were sent through it only in 2015. Thus, Blockchain developers have significant demand in the market.

The Blockchain eliminates the payoff of the middlemen in such monetary transactions. It was the invention of the GUI (Graphical User Interface), which facilitated the common man to access computers in form of desktops. Similarly, the wallet application is the most common GUI for the Blockchain technology. Users make use of the wallet to buy things they want using Bitcoin or any other cryptocurrency.

With traditional transactions, a payment from one person to another involves some kind of intermediary to facilitate the transaction. Let's say Rob wants to transfer £20 to Melanie. He can either give her cash in the form of a £20 note, or he can use some kind of banking app to transfer the money directly to her bank account. In both cases, a bank is the intermediary verifying the transaction: Rob's funds are verified when he takes the money out of a cash machine, or they are verified by the app when he makes the digital transfer. The bank decides if the transaction should go ahead. The bank also holds the record of all transactions made by Rob, and is solely responsible for updating it whenever Rob pays someone or receives money into his account. In other words, the bank holds and controls the ledger, and everything flows through the bank.

That's a lot of responsibility, so it's important that Rob feels he can trust his bank otherwise he would not risk his money with them. He needs to feel confident that the bank will not defraud him, will not lose his money, will not be robbed, and will not disappear overnight. This need for trust has underpinned pretty much every major behaviour and facet of the monolithic finance industry, to the extent that even when it was discovered that banks were being irresponsible with our money during the financial crisis of 2008, the government (another intermediary) chose to bail them out rather than risk destroying the final fragments of trust by letting them collapse.

Blockchains operate differently in one key respect: they are entirely decentralised. There is no central clearing house like a bank, and there is no central ledger held by one entity. Instead, the ledger is distributed across a vast network of computers, called nodes, each of which holds a copy of the entire ledger on their respective hard drives. These nodes are connected to one another via a piece of software called a peer-to-peer (P2P) client, which synchronises data across the network of nodes and makes sure that everybody has the same version of the ledger at any given point in time.

When a new transaction is entered into a blockchain, it is first encrypted using state-of-the-art cryptographic technology. Once encrypted, the transaction is converted to something called a block, which is basically the term used for an encrypted group of new transactions. That block is then sent (or broadcast) into the network of computer nodes, where it is verified by the nodes and, once verified, passed on through the network so that the block can be added to the end of the ledger on everybody's computer, under the list of all previous blocks. This is called the chain, hence the tech is referred to as a blockchain.

Once approved and recorded into the ledger, the transaction can be completed. This is how cryptocurrencies like Bitcoin work.

Accountability And The Removal Of Trust

What are the advantages of this system over a banking or central clearing system? Why would Rob use Bitcoin instead of normal currency?

The answer is trust. As mentioned before, with the banking system it is critical that Rob trusts his bank to protect his money and handle it properly. To ensure this happens, enormous regulatory systems exist to verify the actions of the banks and ensure they are fit for purpose. Governments then regulate the regulators, creating a sort of tiered system of checks whose sole purpose is to help prevent mistakes and bad behaviour. In other words, organizations like the Financial Services Authority exist precisely because banks can't be trusted on their own. And banks frequently make mistakes and misbehave, as we have seen too many times. When you have a single source of authority, power tends to get abused or misused. The trust relationship between people and banks is awkward and precarious: we don't really trust them but we don't feel there is much alternative.

Blockchain systems, on the other hand, don't need you to trust them at all. All transactions (or blocks) in a blockchain are verified by the nodes in the network before being added to the ledger, which means there is no single point of failure and no single approval channel. If a hacker wanted to successfully tamper with the ledger on a blockchain, they would have to simultaneously hack millions of computers, which is almost impossible. A hacker would also be pretty much unable to bring a blockchain network down, as, again, they would need to be able to shut down every single computer in a network of computers distributed around the world.

The encryption process itself is also a key factor. Blockchains like the Bitcoin one use deliberately difficult processes for their verification procedure. In the case of Bitcoin, blocks are verified by nodes performing a deliberately processor- and time-intensive series of calculations, often in the form of puzzles or complex mathematical problems, which mean that verification is neither instant nor accessible. Nodes that do commit the resource to verification of blocks are rewarded with a transaction fee and a bounty of newly-minted Bitcoins. This has the function of both incentivising people to become nodes (because processing blocks like this requires pretty powerful computers and a lot of electricity), whilst also handling the process of generating - or minting - units of the currency. This is referred to as mining, because it involves a considerable amount of effort (by a computer, in this case) to produce a new commodity. It also means that transactions are verified by the most independent way possible, more independent than a government-regulated organisation like the FSA.

This decentralised, democratic and highly secure nature of blockchains means that they can function without the need for regulation (they are self-regulating), government or other opaque intermediary. They work because people don't trust each other, rather than in spite of.

Let the significance of that sink in for a while and the excitement around blockchain starts to make sense.

Smart Contracts

Where things get really interesting is the applications of blockchain beyond cryptocurrencies like Bitcoin. Given that one of the underlying principles of the blockchain system is the secure, independent verification of a transaction, it's easy to imagine other ways in which this type of process can be valuable. Unsurprisingly, many such applications are already in use or development. Some of the best ones are:

Smart contracts (Ethereum): probably the most exciting blockchain development after Bitcoin, smart contracts are blocks that contain code that must be executed in order for the contract to be fulfilled. The code can be anything, as long as a computer can execute it, but in simple terms it means that you can use blockchain technology (with its independent verification, trustless architecture and security) to create a kind of escrow system for any kind of transaction. As an example, if you're a web designer you could create a contract that verifies if a new client's website is launched or not, and then automatically release the funds to you once it is. No more chasing or invoicing. Smart contracts are also being used to prove ownership of an asset such as property or art. The potential for reducing fraud with this approach is enormous.

Cloud storage (Storj): cloud computing has revolutionised the web and brought about the advent of Big Data which has, in turn, kick started the new AI revolution. But most cloud-based systems are run on servers stored in single-location server farms, owned by a single entity (Amazon, Rackspace, Google etc). This presents all the same problems as the banking system, in that you data is controlled by a single, opaque organisation which represents a single point of failure. Distributing data on a blockchain removes the trust issue entirely and also promises to increase reliability as it is so much harder to take a blockchain network down.

Digital identification (ShoCard): two of the biggest issues of our time are identify theft and data protection. With vast centralised services such as Facebook holding so much data about us, and efforts by various developed-world governments to store digital information about their citizens in a central database, the potential for abuse of our personal data is terrifying. Blockchain technology offers a potential solution to this by wrapping your key data up into an encrypted block that can be verified by the blockchain network whenever you need to prove your identity. The applications of this range from the obvious replacement of passports and I.D. cards to other areas such as replacing passwords. It could be huge.

Digital voting: highly topical in the wake of the investigation into Russia's influence on the recent

U.S. election, digital voting has long been suspected of being both unreliable and highly vulnerable to tampering. Blockchain technology offers a way of verifying that a voter's vote was successfully sent while retaining their anonymity. It promises not only to reduce fraud in elections but also to increase general voter turnout as people will be able to vote on their mobile phones. Blockchain technology is still very much in its infancy and most of the applications are a long way from general use. Even Bitcoin, the most established blockchain platform, is subject to huge volatility indicative of its relative newcomer status. However, the potential for blockchain to solve some of the major problems we face today makes it an extraordinarily exciting and seductive technology to follow. These days, technology is scaling newer heights of success at an unbelievably fast pace. One of the latest triumphs in this direction is the evolution of the Blockchain technology. The new technology has greatly influenced the finance sector. In fact, it was initially developed for Bitcoin - the digital currency. But now, it finds its application in a number of other things as well.

How Does The Blockchain Works?

One Bitcoin is a single unit of the Bitcoin (BTC) digital currency, just like a Dollar it has no value by itself, it has value only because we agree to trade goods and services in exchange for a higher amount of the currency under our control and we believe others will do the same.

To keep track of the amount of Bitcoins each of us owns the blockchain uses a ledger, a digital file that keeps track of all Bitcoin transactions.

The ledger file is not stored in a central entity servers, like a bank, or in a single data center. It is distributed across the world via a network of private computers that are both storing data and executing computations. Each of these computers represents a "node" of the blockchain network and has a copy of the ledger file.

If David wants to send Bitcoins to Sandra, he broadcasts a message to the network that says the amount of Bitcoins in his account should go down by 5 BTC, and the amount of Sandra's account should go up by the same quantity. Each node in the network will receive the message and apply the requested transaction to their copy of the ledger, thus updating the account balances.

The fact that the ledger is maintained by a group of connected computers rather than by a centralized entity like a bank has several implications:

While in our bank system we only know our own transactions and account balances, on the blockchain everyone can see everyone's else transactions.

While you can generally trust your bank, the Bitcoin network is distributed and if something goes wrong there is no help desk to call or anyone to sue.

The blockchain system is designed in such a way that no trust is needed, security and reliability are obtained via special mathematical functions and code.

In order to be able to perform transactions on the blockchain, you need a wallet, a program that allows you to store and exchange your Bitcoins. Since only you should be able to spend your Bitcoins, each wallet is protected by a special cryptographic method that uses a unique pair of different but connected keys: a private and a public key.

If a message is encrypted with a specific public key, only the owner of the paired private key will be able to decrypt and read the message. On the other way, if you encrypt a message with your private key, only the paired public key can be used to decrypt it. When David wants to send Bitcoins, he needs to broadcast a message encrypted with the private key of his wallet, so he and only he can spend the Bitcoins he owns as David is the only one to know his own private key necessary to unlock his wallet. Each node in the network can cross check that the transaction request is coming from David by decrypting the transaction request message with the public key of his wallet.

When encrypting a transaction request with your wallet's private key you are generating a digital signature that is used by blockchain computers to double check the source and the authenticity of the transaction. The digital signature is a string of text that is the result of a combination of your transaction request and your private key, therefore it cannot be used for other transactions. If you change a single character in the transaction request message the digital signature will change, so no potential attacker can change your transaction requests or alter the amount of Bitcoins you are sending.

To send bitcoin you need to prove that you own the private key of a specific wallet as you need to use it to encrypt the transaction request message. Please note that since you broadcast the message only after it has been encrypted, you never have to reveal your private key.

Each node in the blockchain is keeping a copy of the ledger. So, how does a node know what's your account balance? The blockchain system doesn't keep track of account balances at all , it only records each and every transaction that is requested. The ledger in fact does not keep track of balances, it only keeps track of every transaction that is broadcasted within the Bitcoin network. To know your wallet balance, you need to analyze and verify all the transactions that ever took place on the whole network connected to your wallet.

This "balance" verification is performed thanks to links to previous transactions. In order to send 10 Bitcoins to John, Mary has to generate a transaction request that includes links to previous incoming transactions whose total balance equals or exceeds 10 Bitcoins. These links are called inputs, nodes in the network will verify that the total amount of these transactions equal or exceeds 10 Bitcoins and that these inputs were not yet spent. In fact, each time you reference inputs in a transaction those are considered not valid in any future transaction. This all is performed automatically in Mary's wallet and double checked by the Bitcoin network nodes, she only sends a 10 BTC transaction to John's wallet using his public key.

So, how can the system trust input transactions and consider them valid? It checks all the previous transactions that are correlated to the wallet you use to send Bitcoins via the references that each one has as inputs. To simplify and speed up the verification process a special record of unspent transactions is kept by the network nodes. Thanks to this security check, it is not possible to double-spend received Bitcoins.

All the code to perform transactions on the Bitcoin network is open source, this means that anyone with a laptop and an internet connection can operate transactions. However, should there be a mistake in the code that is used to broadcast a transaction request message, the associated Bitcoins will be permanently lost. Remember that since the network is distributed, there is no customers support to call nor anyone that could help you restore a lost transaction or your forgotten wallet password. For this reason, if you are interested in transacting on the Bitcoin network it's recommended to use the open source and official version of Bitcoin wallet software (such as Bitcoin Core) and to store your wallet's password or private key in a very safe repository.

Using The Blockchain Technology Has quite Remarkable Benefits:

You have complete control of the value you own, there is no third party that holds your value or that can limit your access to it. The cost to perform a value transaction from and to anywhere in the planet is very low (in the order of a dollar cent fraction). This allows micropayments.

Value can be transferred in few minutes and the transaction can be considered secure in a few hours, not days or weeks.

Since anyone at any time can verify every transaction made on the blockchain, full transparency is granted.

It's possible to leverage the blockchain technology to build decentralized applications that would be able to manage information and value transfer fast and securely.

However, There Are A Few Challenges That Need To Be Addressed:

Transactions can be sent and received anonymously. On one side this preserves the users privacy but on the other allows non legal activity on the network as institutions cannot track users identity.

Even if many exchange platforms are emerging, it's still not that easy to trade bitcoins for goods and services. However, they are becoming more and more popular.

Bitcoin, like many other cryptocurrencies, is very volatile: there aren't that many Bitcoins available in the market and the demand is changing rapidly. Bitcoin price is very effected by large events or announcements in the cryptocurrencies industry.Bitcoin, like many other cryptocurrencies, is very volatile: there aren't that many Bitcoins available in the market and the demand is changing rapidly. Bitcoin price is very effected by large events or announcements in the cryptocurrencies industry.

The technology is still in its infancy. New tools are developed every day to improve the blockchain security stability while offering a broader range of features, tools and services.

Overall, the blockchain technology has the potential to revolutionize several industries from advertising to energy distribution. Its main power lies in its abilities of not requiring trust and being decentralized. Many use cases of this brilliant technology are arising (i.e. the possibility to create a fully decentralized platform that runs smart contracts like Ethereum)

Bitcoin, a money exchange system, pioneered blockchain technology and today, it has more than 8 million accounts and grew by more than 100% per year since it began in 2010. The person or team behind the service is known by the pseudonym Satoshi Nakamoto, but the entity's real identity is cloaked in secrecy.

Everyone Should Know These 14 Things About Blockchains

1 - Blockchains can be public (like the internet) or private (like an intranet).

2 - In terms of its development, blockchain is where the internet was 20 years ago.

3 - Only 0.5% of the world's population is using blockchain today, but 50% or 3.77 billion people use the internet.

4 - There is significant investment by today's tech giants such as IBM and Microsoft in blockchain technology. IBM dedicates $200 million and 1,000 employees to blockchain-powered projects.

5 - The average investment in blockchain projects is $1 million.

6 - Over the last five years, VCs have invested more than $1 billion into blockchain companies.

7 - The global blockchain market is expected to be worth $20 billion by 2024.

8 - 90% of major North American and European banks are exploring blockchain solutions.

9 - Blockchains are highly transparent, because anyone with access to a blockchain can view the entire chain.

10 - Similar to a Google doc, all participants within a network see all changes to the ledger. The ledger is constantly updated and each participant has their own copy of it.

11 - A blockchain is most vulnerable to a breach when it first come online.

12 - 9 out of 10 agree that blockchain will disrupt the banking and financial industry. It is estimated that banks could save $8-12 billion annually if they used blockchain technology.

13 - One-third of C-level executives are considering adopting or are using blockchain technology.

14 - Just like with the internet, there will be jobs that become obsolete. But, there will be new careers that we haven't even dreamed up yet that will be created as a result of the blockchain transformation.

Chapter 5

HOW TO TRADE CRYPTOCURRENCIES

The Basics of Investing in Digital Currencies

Whether it's the idea of cryptocurrencies itself or diversification of their portfolio, people from all walks of life are investing in digital currencies. If you're new to the concept and wondering what's going on, here are some basic concepts and considerations for investment in cryptocurrencies.

What Cryptocurrencies Are Available And How Do I Buy Them?

With a market cap of about $278 billion, Bitcoin is the most established cryptocurrency. Ethereum is second with a market cap of over $74 billion. Besides these two currencies, there are a number of other options as well, including Ripple ($28B), Litecoin ($17B), and MIOTA ($13B).

Being first to market, there are a lot of exchanges for Bitcoin trade all over the world. BitStamp and Coinbase are two well-known US-based exchanges. Bitcoin.de is an established European exchange. If you are interested in trading other digital currencies along with Bitcoin, then a crypto marketplace is where you will find all the digital currencies in one place. Here is a list of exchanges according to their 24-hour trade volume.

What Options Do I Have To Store My Money?

Another important consideration is storage of the coins. One option, of course, is to store it on the exchange where you buy them. However, you will have to be careful in selecting the exchange. The popularity of digital currencies has resulted in many new, unknown exchanges popping up everywhere. Take the time to do your due diligence so you can avoid the scammers.

Another option you have with cryptocurrencies is that you can store them yourself. One of the safest options for storing your investment is hardware wallets. Companies like Ledger allow you store Bitcoins and several other digital currencies as well.

What's The Market Like And How Can I Learn More About It?

The cryptocurrency market fluctuates a lot. The volatile nature of the market makes it more suited for a long-term play.

There are many established news sites that report on digital currencies, including Coindesk, Business Insider, Coin Telegraph, and Cryptocoin News. Besides these sites, there are also many Twitter accounts that tweet about digital currencies, including @BitcoinRTs and @AltCoinCalendar.

Digital currencies aim to disrupt the traditional currency and commodity market. While these currencies still have a long way to go, the success of

Bitcoins and Ethereum have proven that there is genuine interest in the concept. Understanding the basics of cryptocurrency investment will help you start in the right way.

Types Of Cryptocurrency Wallets And Their Overall Security Aspect

There exists various types of cryptocurrency wallets to allow users store and access their digital currencies in different ways. The question that is relevant in this context is how far are these wallets secure. Before taking up the security aspect, it is helpful to understand the various types or varieties of cryptocurrency wallets that exist today.

Cryptocurrency wallet: Types and varieties

These wallets can broadly be classified in 3 categories:

- Software wallets

- Hardware wallets and

- Paper wallets

Cryptocurrency software wallets can again be subdivided into desktop, online and mobile wallets.

Desktop software wallets: These wallets are meant to be downloaded and installed on desktop PCs and laptops. This particular variety offers the highest level of security though their accessibility is limited only to the computer in which they are installed. Moreover, in case, if the computer gets hacked or is virus-infected, there's a possibility that one may lose all his or her money.

Online software wallets: This range of cryptocurrency wallets run on the Cloud. Thus, they can easily be accessed from any computing device and from any geographical location. Apart from accessibility convenience, this type of digital wallets store the private keys online. The keys are even controlled by third-parties; this makes them easily vulnerable to hacking and theft.

Mobile software wallets: Unlike the two other varieties, mobile software wallets run on smartphones through an app. These can easily be used everywhere, including retail stores and malls. This range of the wallets is usually much simpler and smaller compared to the normal desktop ones to accommodate with the very limited space on mobile handsets.

Difference Between Hardware And Software Wallets

Hardware digital wallets vary from the software ones on the aspect of storing a user's private keys. The hardware wallets store the user keys in a hardware device (for example, the USB). Thus, as the keys are stored offline, these wallets offer an added security. Moreover, hardware wallets are easily compatible with many online interfaces and can also handle different currencies. This variety of cryptocurrency wallets is also easy to make transactions with. As a user, you just need to plug in the device to any computer, which is connected to the web before entering a PIN, transfer the currency and just confirm the transaction. Your digital currency is kept offline by the hardware wallets and thus, the risk factor or security concern is also much lesser.

Paper digital wallets: This range of digital wallets is also user-friendly and ensures a high-level of security. The term "paper wallet" just refers to the hardcopy printout of a user's both public and private keys. However, considering the instances, it can also refer to a software application meant to generate the keys securely before printing.

Paper Wallets - Using paper wallets is relatively somewhat easier. In order to transfer any cryptocurrency to your paper wallet, just transfer the funds from the software wallet to the public address, which your paper wallet displays. Similarly, when you want to spend or withdraw your money, just transfer the funds from the paper wallet to your software wallet. This procedure is popularly referred to as 'sweeping'.

Sweeping can be done either manually, by entering the private keys or scanning the QR code on a paper wallet.

How Secure Cryptocurrency Wallets Are

Different varieties of digital wallets offer different levels of security. The security aspect mainly depends on two factors:

The Type Of Wallet You Use - Hardware, Paper, Online, Desktop Or Mobile A chosen service provider

It doesn't require mentioning, it is much safer to keep the currencies in offline environment, as compared to online. There's just no way to ignore the security measures, irrespective of the wallet one has chosen. If you lose your private keys, all the money kept in the wallet will be gone away from your hands. On the other hand, if the wallet gets hacked or you transfer funds to a scammer, it won't be possible to reverse the transaction nor reclaim that money.

Investing in cryptocurrency is a smart business idea and for that, using a suitable wallet is inevitable. You just need to be bit cautious to ensure safety and security aspect to your fund transfers and transactions.

Chapter 6

WHAT CRYPTOCURRENCIES ARE GOOD TO INVEST IN

Bitcoin has soared, even past one gold-ounce. There are also new cryptocurrencies on the market, which is even more surprising which brings cryptocoins' worth up to more than one hundred billion. On the other hand, the longer term cryptocurrency-outlook is somewhat of a blur. There are squabbles of lack of progress among its core developers which make it less alluring as a long term investment and as a system of payment.

Bitcoin

Still the most popular, Bitcoin is the cryptocurrency that started all of it. It is currently the biggest market cap at around $41 billion and has been around for the past 8 years. Around the world, Bitcoin has been widely used and so far there is no easy to exploit weakness in the method it works. Both as a payment system and as a stored value, Bitcoin enables users to easily receive and send bitcoins. The concept of the blockchain is the basis in which Bitcoin is based. It is necessary to understand the blockchain concept to get a sense of what the cryptocurrencies are all about.

To put it simply, blockchain is a database distribution that stores every network transaction as a data-chunk called a "block." Each user has blockchain copies so when Alice sends 1 bitcoin to Mark, every person on the network knows it.

Litecoin

One alternative to Bitcoin, Litecoin attempts to resolve many of the issues that hold Bitcoin down. It is not quite as resilient as Ethereum with its value derived mostly from adoption of solid users. It pays to note that Charlie Lee, ex-Googler leads Litecoin.

He is also practicing transparency with what he is doing with Litecoin and is quite active on Twitter.

Litecoin was Bitcoin's second fiddle for quite some time but things started changing early in the year of 2017. First, Litecoin was adopted by Coinbase along with Ethereum and Bitcoin. Next, Litecoin fixed the Bitcoin issue by adopting the technology of Segregated Witness. This gave it the capacity to lower transaction fees and do more. The deciding factor, however, was when Charlie Lee decided to put his sole focus on Litecoin and even left Coinbase, where're he was the Engineering Director, just for Litecoin. Due to this, the price of Litecoin rose in the last couple of months with its strongest factor being the fact that it could be a true alternative to Bitcoin.

Ethereum

Vitalik Buterin, superstar programmer thought up Ethereum, which can do everything Bitcoin is able to do. However its purpose, primarily, is to be a platform to build decentralized applications. The blockchains are where the differences between the two lie. Basically, the blockchain of Bitcoin records a contract-type, one that states whether funds have been moved from one digital address to another address. However, there is significant expansion with Ethereum as it has a more advanced language script and has a more complex, broader scope of applications.

Projects began to sprout on top of Ethereum when developers began noticing its better qualities. Through token crowd sales, some have even raised dollars by the millions and this is still an ongoing trend even to this day. The fact that you can build wonderful things on the Ethereum platform makes it almost like the internet itself. This caused a skyrocketing in the price so if you purchased a hundred dollars' worth of Ethereum early this year, it would not be valued at almost $3000.

Monero

Monero aims to solve the issue of anonymous transactions. Even if this currency was perceived to be a method of laundering money, Monero aims to change this. Basically, the difference between Monero and Bitcoin is that Bitcoin features a transparent blockchain with every transaction public and recorded. With Bitcoin, anyone can see how and where the money was moved. There is some somewhat imperfect anonymity on Bitcoin, however. In contrast, Monero has an opaque rather than transparent transaction method. No one is quite sold on this method but since some folks love privacy for whatever purpose, Monero is here to stay.

Zcash

Not unlike Monero, Zcash also aims to solve the issues that Bitcoin has. The difference is that rather than being completely transparent, Monero is only partially public in its blockchain style. Zcash also aims to solve the problem of anonymous transactions. After all, no every person loves showing how much money they actually spent on memorabilia by Star Wars. Thus, the conclusion is that this type of cryptocoin really does have an audience and a demand, although it's hard to point out which cryptocurrency that focuses on privacy will eventually come out on top of the pile.

Bancor

Also known as a "smart token," Bancor is the new generation standard of cryptocurrencies which can hold more than one token on reserve. Basically, Bancor attempts to make it easy to trade, manage and create tokens by increasing their level of liquidity and letting them have a market price that is automated. At the moment, Bancor has a product on the front-end that includes a wallet and the creation of a smart token. There are also features in the community such as stats, profiles and discussions. In a nutshell, the protocol of Bancor enables the discovery of a price built-in as well as a mechanism for liquidity for smart contractual tokens through a mechanism of innovative reserve. Through smart contract, you can instantly liquidate or purchase any of the tokens within the reserve of Bancor. With Bancor, you can create new cryptocoins with ease. Now who wouldn't want that?

Eos

Another competitor of Ethereum, Eos promises to solve the scaling issue of Ethereum through the provision of a set of tools that are more robust to run and create apps on the platform.

Tezos

An alternative to Ethereum, Tezos can be consensually upgraded without too much effort. This new blockchain is decentralized in the sense that it is self-governing through the establishment of a digital true commonwealth. It facilitates the mathematical technique called formal verification and has security-boosting features of the most financially weighed, sensitive smart contract. Definitely a great investment in the months to come.

Verdict

It is incredibly hard to predict which Bitcoin in the list will become the next superstar. However, user adoption has always be one key success factor when it came to cryptocurrencies. Both Ethereum and Bitcoin have this and even if there is a lot of support from early adopters of every cryptocurrency in the list, some have yet to prove their staying power. Nonetheless, these are the ones to invest in and watch out for in the coming months.

Chapter 7

INCREDIBLE BENEFITS OF THE CRYPTOCURRENCY

Over the past few years, people have been talking a lot about cryptocurrency. At first, this business sounded scary but people started developing trust in it. You may have heard of Ether and Bitcoin. They both are crypto currencies and use the Blockchain Technology for highest security possible. Nowadays, these currencies are available in several types.

How Can Cryptocurrency Help You?

As far as fraud is concerned, this type of currency can't be faked as it's in digital form and can't be reversed or counterfeited unlike the credit cards.

Immediate Settlement

Buying real property involves third parties, such as lawyers and notary. So, delays can occur and extra costs may incur. On the other hand, Bitcoin contracts are designed and enforced in order to include or exclude third parties. The transactions are quick and settlements can be made instantly.

Lower Fees

Typically, there is no transaction fee if you want to exchange Bitcoin or any other currency. For verifying a transaction, there are minors who get paid by the network. Although there is zero transaction fee, most buyers or sellers hire the services of a third-party, such as Coinbase for the creation and maintenance of their wallets. If you don't know, these services function just like Paypal that offers a web-based exchange system.

Identification Of Theft

Your merchant gets your full credit line when you provide them with your credit card. This is true even if the transaction amount is very small. Actually, what happens is that credit cards work based on a "pull" system where the online store pulls the required amount from the account associated with the card. On the other hand, the digital currencies feature a "push" mechanism where the account holder sends only the amount required without any additional information. So, there is no chance of theft.

Open Access

According to statistics, there are around 2.2 billion people who use the Internet but not all of them have access to the conventional exchange. So, they can use the new form of payment method.

Decentralization

As far as decentralization is concerned, an international computer network called Blockchain technology manages the database of Bitcoin. In other words, Bitcoin is under the administration of the network, and there is no central authority. In other words, the network works on a peer-to-peer based approach.

Recognition

Since cryptocurrency is not based on the exchange rates, transaction charges or interest rates, you can use it internationally without suffering from any problems. So, you can save a lot of time and money. In other words, Bitcoin and other currencies like this are recognized all over the world. You can count on them.

So, if you have been looking for a way to invest your extra money, you can consider investing in Bitcoin. You can either become a miner or investor. However, make sure you know what you are doing. Safety is not an issue but other things are important to be kept in mind.

Buying And Spending Cryptocurrency

When it comes to buying and selling cryptocurrency, there are more options available than you may think.

For buying, the individual cryptocurrency websites can advise you on how to purchase some of their precious digital tokens, or you can get them through cryptocurrency exchange websites.

If you are looking to purchase Bitcoin, your options are even more plentiful as there are Bitcoin ATM machines placed throughout the world. These ATMs work similarly to a regular machine, except rather than a bank card you will need to use government-issued identification on a scanner to make a withdrawal.

Since the first ATM being installed in Austin, Texas in February 2014, there were 1189 Bitcoin ATMs across the world as of May 2017, with three being installed per day.

You can find a Bitcoin ATM near you, and purchase Bitcoins for cash or withdraw cash for Bitcoins.

There are many high street and local retailers who now accept Bitcoin as currency in exchange for their goods or services, making the cryptocurrency surprisingly accessible.

Chapter 8

THE FUTURE OF CRYPTOCURRENCY

There are two sides to every subject, and the same goes for cryptocurrency. Negative is a massive bubble of unofficial money with perceived value that exceeds actual value. Positive is a huge opportunity, not only in cryptocurrencies, but also with the underlying network of blockchain technology and how it can affect businesses globally.

Arics technology provides best web hosting service that is an important part of your online business. It doesn't matter whether you have a small or big business website, you must have a dedicated server hosting with high reliability and very least downtime. Keeping this in mind we at Arics Technology provide a secure,reliable & powerful hosting at affordable prices.

In every business we do, we always have risks to lose our money, but we invest to win. When you going to invest, you need to study where you going to send your money and make sure to know the risks to lose it or the chances to increment your capital.

CONCLUSION

Cryptocurrency is fast becoming a true rival to traditional currency across the world. The digital currency is available to purchase in many different places, making it accessible to everyone, and with retailers accepting Bitcoin it could be a sign that money as we know it is about to go through a major change.

The total market capitalization of cryptocurrencies, as of September 2017, is worth more than 100 billion USD, and currently has a record high daily volume of larger than 6 billion USD.

Making currency decentralized is very appealing within the world of hacking and tampering of which we live. If protecting our money means taking it away from the centralized banks, it's highly likely that the market capitalization of cryptocurrencies will continue to grow. As more retailers start accepting cryptocurrency, and more cryptocurrencies come into circulation, people have more choice than ever when it comes to managing their own money which is something which is pulling more people into the cryptocurrency world than ever before.

ABOUT THE AUTHOR

My name Raymundo Ramirez from Guanajuato México, I love to read and write books, play soccer, basket ball, hear all kind of music, exercise my body frequently and try to live my life happy with my family. I been living in Orange County Ca. Since 1986.

OTHERS AUTHOR EBOOKS ARE

- The Law of Atraction
- How to Become a Police Officer
- Leadership in Action
- The Guide to the Network Marketing
- How to Promote Your Business Online
- How to Create a Successfull Web Page
- Home Business
- Why to Write an Ebook
- The Ghostwriter World
- Multinivel
- Piensa y Triunfaras... and more.

You find these titles in: **play.google.com/store**

Click on search, write raymundo ramirez and you there.

Notes

www.ingramcontent.com/pod-product-compliance
Lightning Source LLC
Chambersburg PA
CBHW031445210526
45464CB00005B/2331